Contents

Page

DISCLAIMER . . . . *ii*

FOREWORD . . . . *v*

ABOUT THE AUTHOR . . . . *vii*

SUMMARY . . . . *ix*

ACKNOWLEDGMENTS . . . . *xi*

LEARNING HOW TO FIGHT TOGETHER: THE BRITISH
EXPERIENCE WITH JOINT AIR-LAND WARFARE   1

    Origins of the Air-Land Debate   5

    Political Wrangling between the Independent
      Air Force and Army/Royal Air Force
      during the Interwar Years   8

    The Battle for France, 1940   10

    The Evolution of Air-Land Technique   11

    North Africa: The Adoption and Refinement
      of a New Air-Land Technique   14

    Success without Harmony: British Air-Land
      Co-operation by the End of the War   25

    Back to Afghanistan and Contemporary
      Air-Land Integration   27

    Enduring Themes and Contemporary Relevance   29

NOTES   32

ABBREVIATIONS   43

Acknowledgments

I would like to thank Dr. Daniel Mortensen, chief of research, Air Force Research Institute at Air University, and Mr. Eugene Moseley Jr., group manager, Northrop Grumman IT-Defense Group, for their personal encouragement and the financial support given to me to produce this research paper. Academic research that aims to contribute to public policy debates can often fall between two stools: academic bodies too often discount the work because it is not published in their preferred journals, and public institutions sometimes question the relevance of opinions proffered by an academic as opposed to a practitioner. Thankfully, the United States Air Force has a much broader and more enlightened view on such matters, and has encouraged the widest possible academic discourse so that those who produce public policy are better informed on the choices open to them. In this respect, I also want to thank Prof. Matthew Uttley, dean of academic studies, KCL at the JSCSC, for his ongoing support for policy-relevant academic research.

Learning How to Fight Together

The British Experience with
Joint Air-Land Warfare

Operation Herrick IV is the name that the British armed forces gave to their operations against the Taliban and other militant forces in Helmand Province, Afghanistan, during the summer of 2006.[1] It was a difficult operation, and August was a particularly difficult month. The combination of a very harsh environment and a fanatically determined enemy, unwilling to give up ground and willing to die protecting it, proved to be a significant challenge for the British expeditionary air and land forces. Wing Cdr Ian Duguid, a veteran Harrier pilot and the commanding officer of the Royal Air Force's (RAF) IV Army Co-operation Squadron, said: "I have been flying for 14 years and nothing has compared with this for the intensity of operations undertaken."[2] In August, Duguid's Harriers attacked up to 12 targets per day and fired 426 CRV7 ground-attack rockets. They fired only 58 of these same ground-attack rockets in July. Air support was an essential force multiplier for the army on the ground as it pressed on with its offensive against the Taliban fighters and their strongholds.

In an attempt to make sense of his combat experience, Maj Jamie Loden, commanding officer of A Company, 3rd Battalion, The Parachute Regiment (3 PARA)—the main United Kingdom (UK) battle group in Herrick IV—sent a deeply reflective e-mail to a fellow army officer. It would prove to be the beginning of an e-mail exchange that ignited a bitter public row between the army and the RAF over air-land integration in current operations. Loden was highly critical of the RAF's ineffectiveness in Afghanistan, stating: "From my point of view controlling and directing air, arty [artillery] and mors [mortars] is the best way to influence the battle. The RAF have [sic] been utterly utterly useless [during operations against the Taliban]. In contrast the USAF have [sic] been fantastic, and I would take an A-10 over Eurofighter any day."[3] The content of this e-mail was leaked to a number of British broadcasters and news organisations, and not surprisingly, it made national and international

1

headline news. It also led to a series of immediate denials by senior army and RAF officers eager to emphasise the close and effective co-operation that existed between the two services deployed on current operations in Afghanistan and elsewhere. Even the chief of the General Staff, Gen Sir Richard Dannatt, was drawn into the fray, conceding that some frontline army officers were being "irresponsible." Unfortunately, however, Loden's criticisms were not just the intemperate words of one angry and demoralised soldier. Rather they reflect a very long and tortuous struggle between Britain's soldiers and airmen over who should control aircraft on the battlefield. They also hint at the protracted difficulties often associated with the acceptance and implementation of new and innovative ideas in large, established institutions. At the heart of the challenge facing the army and the RAF in their efforts to improve air-land integration is the difficult task of matching the different means by which air and land forces support the conduct of expeditionary operations. Both Major Loden's outburst and the uncomfortably anxious manner by which his criticisms were dismissed by senior officers in the army and the RAF suggest that there remains a lot to be done before Britain's current operational commanders can be assured of close coordination and effective integration across components for decisive joint action on and above the contemporary battlespace.[4]

Bitterness amongst British soldiers over what they have perceived to be "negligible and sporadic RAF fighter cover and bomber support" has been a common feature of all British military operations since the First World War, when combat aircraft first appeared over the battlefield. On many occasions it has also led a number of senior army officers to call for wholesale changes to British air policy, particularly with regard to the "independent" air force providing the army with air support on expeditionary operations. Most soldiers believe their air-support requirements will only be met when army commanders have "air resources at their disposal which are adequate for the operations in hand."[5] The same soldiers are certain that this will happen only when all army commanders receive full control over whatever air resources are allocated to them, along with the unquestioned right to order the RAF to undertake any and all other tasks that are required in support of the land forces and the land operation. In short, most

2

soldiers want their own organic air for tactical actions whilst they tend to ignore the larger strategic and operational questions concerning national and theatre objectives and the appropriate allocation of high-value yet finite air assets.

Brig Cyrus Greenslade summed up the views of many of his fellow army officers with unreserved honesty when he said "it is axiomatic that it is impractical to attempt to fight without there being adequate air forces under the operational control of the Army."[6] He, like many soldiers, desired suitable close-support aircraft under the army commander's direct command and control. Greenslade did not base his analysis on the shortcomings of air-land integration in recent operations in Afghanistan or Iraq. He was, in fact, one of more than one-third of a million British and Allied servicemen to be evacuated from Dunkirk in June 1940 as the German blitzkrieg surged to victory in the battle for France. In the weeks that followed the Allied defeat, Greenslade was also one of a number of British army and RAF officers who studied the recent fighting in search of lessons for the future. By the end of July 1940, both the army and the RAF understood that the ability to conduct fully integrated air-land operations was one of the key prerequisites to winning the war. But just how the two services were going to establish a new approach to the planning and conduct of successful air-land operations was something the soldiers and the airmen could not agree on.

For Air Marshal Sir W. Sholto Douglas the solution to the problem was simple: "All you need is the willingness to co-operate and good signals."[7] Breaking down years of mistrust and misunderstanding, however, would prove to be much more difficult than the introduction of either new doctrine or new technology at the battlefront. The two services had to overcome distinctive cultural differences in the way they conceptualised their respective operations and the way they fought their battles against the formidable Wehrmacht. They also had to develop greater empathy for each other and foster real mutual respect that embraced rather than rejected their differences as sister services. All of this takes time, and time is not a luxury for a nation or its armed forces when fully engaged in war, especially when it is a war of national survival.

The process by which the British Army and the RAF overcame these difficulties between June 1940 and the spring of

1943 is one of the more remarkable stories to emerge out of the Second World War.[8] Joint command and signals experiments in the UK along with successful battlefield experience in North Africa combined with the strategic and tactical acumen of Air Marshals Sir Arthur Tedder and Sir Arthur Coningham, the active co-operation of Gen Bernard Montgomery, and the political authority of Winston Churchill to produce a uniquely British system that afforded the most comprehensive, effective, and flexible air support provided by any air force in 1942. Under Gen Dwight D. Eisenhower's initiative, America's floundering armies in North Africa eventually rejected their wartime arrangements and practices and copied the new British method of army co-operation and air support.[9] US air planners and strategists, drawing on their own very sound prewar theoretical studies and principles, further refined the British Western Desert Air Force (WDAF) system for the combined Anglo-American forces that fought so successfully in Italy and Northwest Europe. Neither new doctrine nor new technology alone can account for the stunning success Anglo-American forces achieved in their provision of effective air support by the later stages of the Second World War. Rather, as Douglas suggested during those bleak summer months in 1940, good communication and the willingness to co-operate proved to be the twin factors that accounted for the operational success achieved.

This study critically examines joint air-land warfare through a historical case study. It looks at the British experience in the two world wars, tracing the obstacles to providing effective joint army-air support at the beginning of the Second World War and illustrating the way these difficulties were eventually overcome by the spring of 1943. In terms of contemporary relevance, this study identifies key enduring lessons (or first principles) for the successful conduct of joint air-land operations. Finally, it concludes with a brief reexamination of the issues behind the British infantry commander's harsh criticism of the RAF in Afghanistan, linking where possible the problems and the solutions of the past with contemporary concerns and impediments to effective air-land integration. This is achieved by addressing a number of the key contemporary questions: What are the army's current grievances over air support? How are they different from or similar to past concerns? Why has effective co-operation between the army and the RAF proved to be so difficult and so illusory? What is being done about this deleterious state of affairs today? And why, despite the fact that the British armed forces have operated a Joint Services Command and Staff College since 1997, do middle-ranking officers, particularly from the army, still lack essential empathy for the other services—a key prerequisite for effective joint operations? By looking back into the not-so-distant past, we may unlock some of the answers to a number of the current problems in providing effective air-land integration in today's complex and ever-changing operating environment.

Origins of the Air-Land Debate

The origins of the British Army's problems in obtaining effective air support began even before Britain had an established air service. A powerful and influential group of generals at the War Office, led by Gen Sir William Nicholson, chief of the Imperial General Staff (CIGS), believed that no type of aeronautical device—dirigible, balloon, glider, or aeroplane—would be of much use to the army.[10] During the summer of 1908, Nicholson shared his emphatic position on the uselessness of military aviation with the British press. It was a judgment that would be disproved with cruel completeness in less than 10 years' time. Nonetheless, Nicholson's antipathy to military aviation set a standard at the War Office that too many future CIGSs and other senior army officers have all too readily and cheerfully emulated.[11]

Despite General Nicholson's rejection of military aviation, the British government pressed on with its desire to establish an air force to support the army and the Royal Navy.[12] Lord Haldane, the secretary of state for war and chairman of the Standing Sub-Committee on the Committee of Imperial Defence on Aerial Navigation, justified his decision with a warning that air forces might play an important role in a future war, and that Britain required an air force that was capable of concentrating its resources for decisive engagements either on land or at sea as the circumstances of the conflict dictated.[13] In May 1912, Haldane therefore recommended the establishment of a centralised aerial service, with a military wing, a naval wing, and a central flying school that could be used to support either the army or the Royal Navy in future operations.[14] Haldane's vision of a flexible, centrally controlled air force would eventually become one of the fundamental principles of the future RAF, but in 1912 it was a concept that fell on the barren ground of an army versus Royal Navy dispute over who should develop the new air service, how military aviation should be controlled, and for what purposes it should be used. Finding this joint enquiry to be too difficult, the two services opted to develop their aviation independently and without further reference to the other. When war between the great European powers began in August 1914, Britain's army and the Royal Navy joined the fight with their own respective air forces, the Royal Flying Corps (RFC) and the Royal Naval Air Service (RNAS).

Small and late in forming, the RFC that accompanied the British Expeditionary Force (BEF) to France consisted of only four squadrons of some 50 aircraft. Left behind in England were another 70 planes of assorted types of which only half were fit to fly.[15] Yet despite this inauspicious beginning, British military aviation, and the army's interest in it, developed and expanded rapidly during the course of the war.[16] By 1916 military aircraft had already performed all of the basic operational roles—minus heavy lift and rotary wing—that would be developed by air forces in the years to come. RFC aircraft were employed on reconnaissance missions, artillery observation, escort and interceptor missions, air-to-air combat, bombing and strafing enemy troops and positions, close air support, direct air support, indirect support, fighter sweeps and air superiority work, and independent strategic bombing.[17] The unprecedented expansion of combat tasks for aircraft over the western front exerted considerable pressure on aircraft manufacturers to produce more and better machines; it also challenged army commanders to use their finite number of aircraft more economically and effectively. Later on in the war, French and German military aviation developed specialised aircraft and squadrons, particularly for ground attack and army support operations.[18] British policy, however, differed sharply from that of the continental powers. Maj Gen Hugh Trenchard, head of the RFC in France throughout most of the war and later the chief of the Air Staff, RAF, argued in favour of a policy that re-

6

jected specialisation and emphasised instead speed of response, flexibility of application, and concentration of maximum force at critical times and points in a battle. Britain's young aviators had learnt through trial and error that all air operations, and especially those in support of the army, were more effective when first air superiority was attained over the battle area. They also recognised that a system of centralised command and control was a necessary prerequisite to attaining air superiority.[19] Achieving these conditions, however, had not been possible in the RFC on a regular basis.

Early command and control arrangements in the RFC reflected the army commander's concerns and desires. The army viewed aircraft as auxiliary forces, similar to artillery and the new tanks, which were attached to army formations at the front and placed under the army commander's direct control. On average one squadron of aircraft was attached to each army corps. Decentralised command and control negated concentration of force and thus prevented Britain's air forces from exercising a strategic impact on the battlefield. But this was not their purpose in army planning. The army used aircraft as "flying artillery" to attack enemy guns and strong points at the forefront of the battlefield in order to help the infantry advance and achieve a breakthrough. Under this system air forces were subordinate to the army's tactical objectives, and senior army commanders were not concerned with the wider application of air forces outside of their own narrow battle area.[20] This, in part, was one of the major reasons for the creation of the Royal Air Force in 1918.[21]

As the British Army struggled to find a solution to trench warfare and the grim stalemate on the western front, army officers increasingly narrowed their focus on military aviation to close air support—a ground attack role in the immediate battle zone. They wrongly believed that more close support would enable them to achieve the thus far unattainable breakthrough, and therefore pursued its development to the exclusion of all other forms of combat aviation. RFC and later RAF leaders despaired at the short-sightedness shown by their former army colleagues and, with the benefit of a growing sense of air-mindedness, espoused a yet unwritten doctrine that emphasised a more strategic application of airpower centred on air superiority, interdiction, and long-range bombing. The Battle of Amiens, in August

1918, was the first mass experiment using aircraft under centralised control in a land battle. It also was the first time that air and land commanders worked together planning a battle. In all previous British offensives, air commanders had executed the army commanders' plans without being included in their construction. Though only a qualified success, Amiens demonstrated the enormous potential that air forces had to isolate a battlefield and make a decisive impact on operations taking place on the ground.[22] The airmen understood exactly what the army was trying to do because they had taken the trouble to find out at the planning stage. During the battle they were able to coordinate their air actions within an integrated air-land battle plan that succeeded in producing the desired operational effects. Air-mindedness was leading directly to a new concept of airpower, which, Trenchard confidently and correctly concluded, had the ability to exert both strategic influence and a decisive operational effect on the conduct of war and campaigns in the future. It was also a concept that the soldiers neither accepted nor made any effort to study and understand.[23] Diverging opinions between airmen and soldiers over the proper employment of aircraft in war soon became the focal point of increasingly bitter disputes between the two services.

Political Wrangling between the Independent Air Force and Army/Royal Air Force during the Interwar Years

After the war, extensive analysis of the use and misuse of air forces led Britain's airmen to establish a set of first principles of air warfare—offensive initiative, air superiority, concentration of force, and the need for centralised command and control—principles which served them well in their development of theory and doctrine throughout the interwar years and the Second World War.[24] Their advocacy of these principles and their advancement of the concept of "airpower" during the early 1920s, however, exacerbated severely strained relations with the army and the Royal Navy, relations that had steadily deteriorated due to deep postwar cuts in the annual defence budgets. During these formative years, the RAF battled against the forces of military reaction for its very life.[25] In RAF circles the story is often told in mythological form and acted out in pantomime. The air force was the beleaguered maiden, the army and the navy were the dragon and its twisted mate, and Lord Trenchard was the holy knight Saint George.[26] Throughout the interwar period, both the army and the Royal Navy viewed the Independent Air Force as an aberration of the last war and wanted it broken up with a view to returning the tactical air wings (army and navy) to the older services. Trenchard remained defiant. He was determined to keep the RAF one and indivisible. His reasoning for this was based on real fears that neither the War Office nor the Admiralty had either the aptitude or the means to advance the development of airpower properly. In the 1920s "properly" meant offensive airpower: long-range bombers and strategic bombing, not army co-operation or fighters for air defence.

Trenchard was convinced that the nation that considered and developed its air forces "as an auxiliary arm to the older services" would "suffer a rude awakening if faced by a nation which has recognised that the air may become a primary medium of war and has developed its airpower accordingly."[27] Strongly emphasising the offensive nature of air warfare, Trenchard and the Air Staff concentrated on developing their theory of strategic bombing. But without any real enemy to worry about in the 1920s, it was "air control" in the trouble spots of the empire that preserved the independence of the RAF. Imperial policing provided substantial financial savings for the British government and in so doing also secured the RAF's future as an independent service with its unique contribution to the defence of the United Kingdom—strategic bombing.[28]

Trenchard's success in securing a future for the "third service" was purchased at a high price. "There was hardly an area of contact between the [army and the RAF]," wrote Derek Waldie, a historian of the interwar period, "where there was not, at best, friction, or, at worst, open hostility."[29] Parsimonious defence budgets, a severe lack of resources, and an absence of "good will" made it next to impossible for the three services to develop new doctrines, never mind co-operative or joint doctrines that incorporated the most recent technologies and theories of war. Throughout the 1920s and most of the 1930s, the three services went their own separate ways planning and preparing to defend Britain and the empire in the unlikely event of a major war. Joint air-land training exercises were seldom held. When they were, too often they highlighted the different approaches of the two services and emphasised the chasm that existed between the army and the RAF over command arrangements and the proper application of air forces in support of a land battle.[30] When war broke out again in Europe in September 1939, Britain's armed forces were not only underequipped for battle, they were woefully unprepared for the close cooperation that was demanded by modern joint and combined warfare in three dimensions.

The Battle for France, 1940

The BEF and RAF that went to France in 1939 were two very different forces, with equally different obligations and objectives. Initially, the BEF was a single corps of two divisions. It took up positions on the left flank of the Anglo-French line between the Seventh and First French Armies on the Franco-Belgian border. RAF deployment consisted of the Advanced Air Striking Force (AASF) and the air component of the field force, which had a number of strategic responsibilities beyond that of providing direct support for the BEF.[31] In addition to the AASF and the air component, the whole of Bomber Command was available to support the Allied armies if required by changes in the strategic situation. These arrangements did not satisfy Gen John Gort, commander in chief (C-in-C) of the BEF; Leslie Hore-Belisha, the secretary of state for war; or Gen Edmund Ironside, the CIGS. The army wanted air forces under its direct command rather than "merely in support."[32] Air and ground training exercises in France had also exposed an overly complicated and unwieldy command structure. The Air Ministry too was eager to improve the existing command and organisational arrangements for the provision of air support. Accordingly, the Air Staff created a single air command, British Air Forces in France (BAFF), with Air Marshal Arthur Barratt as its air officer commander in chief (AOC-in-C). Barratt further proposed the creation of a joint army-air headquarters, with his own headquarters side-by-side on the same site as the C-in-C's BEF headquarters. General Gort, however, thought little of Barratt's suggestion and dismissed it as being "unnecessary."[33]

The calamitous Battle of France convinced the soldiers that they had been right all along: an army required its own aircraft if it was to have any chance of success in a war against a first-rate opponent such as the Wehrmacht. Furthermore, the War Office claimed that the army required its own specialised air forces, consisting of a fighter umbrella for defence and dive-bombers for close offensive support, suballotted to ground commanders at both corps and divisional levels. The Air Ministry disagreed. Whilst recent events in France had revealed a number of defects in the BAFF's system of air support, there was one glaring weakness that overshadowed all of the others, and that was numerical inferiority. There were never enough RAF aircraft in France to perform the many and varied tasks envisaged for them, and substantial reinforcement was never a practical option. Fighter squadrons were in short supply, and, in any case, home-air-defence requirements tended to dominate decisions taken regarding the deployment of Britain's comparatively small air force.[34] Effective air support, cited the airmen, was dependent on a high degree of air superiority. Achieving this superiority demanded an air force superior in strength to the enemy air force opposite: a unified air force consisting of bombers, fighters, communication, and transport aircraft all under centralised air command with the flexibility to switch from one task to another as strategic and operational circumstances dictated. It would not be vast numbers of specialised support aircraft tethered to the ground forces. Lack of aircraft accounted for the reverses suffered—not, as the War Office wrongly believed, the RAF's air-support system. More aircraft, exhorted the airmen, along with more mobility for air forces on the ground to advance and withdraw with the army as well as better communications to coordinate the efforts of both services in the field, were required to turn defeat into victory.[35]

The Evolution of Air-Land Technique

During the late summer and autumn of 1940, the two services searched for answers to the air-support dilemma.[36] The War Office established a special committee under Gen Sir

11

William Bartholomew, long renowned for his enmity toward the RAF, to study the problem and make recommendations for a new policy.[37] After hearing oral evidence from a number of senior army officers and an airman who had fought in France, the committee recommended that the army receive its own independent air arm.[38] It was the RAF system that was at fault. The conclusion was hardly a surprise. It did, however, reveal the parochial nature of army thinking and the failure of the army's frontline commanders to comprehend the character of the newly combined air and armoured warfare that had just defeated them.

Whilst the army was blaming others for its battlefield defeats, the Air Staff promoted a series of joint army-air signals experiments to determine the most appropriate methods for developing close co-operation between air and ground forces fighting a land battle. Conducted in Northern Ireland from 5 September through 28 October 1940, these investigations produced one of the most momentous developments of the war. Group Capt A. H. Wann and Lt Col John Woodall devised a system of joint army-air command in the field supported by a sophisticated signals network that linked forward ground troops with a combined battlefield headquarters and advanced airfields.[39] Once fully developed, the air-support controls (ASC) provided British air and land forces with the organisational and technical means to direct and manage effective air support for both offensive and defensive operations.

Around the same time that the ASC system was being developed in the UK, a similar system—one that emphasised colocated army-air headquarters and a discrete, sophisticated signals network that linked forward and rear airfields with the joint army-air headquarters as well as with deployed divisions and brigades of the army—was the subject of a number of army/RAF experiments in North Africa. Uncertainty over the immediate benefits that these new ideas and operating procedures might bring to army-air co-operation in the field led to inevitable delays in the army accepting and subsequently making full and effective use of the new air-support system. In addition, battlefield experience—particularly the army's all-too-regular defeats at the hands of Col-Gen Erwin Rommel's Afrika Korps—provided a harsh test for the new air-support theories as well as more ammunition for acrimonious debates between soldiers and airmen over the best arrangements for future army-air co-operation. Once fully developed, however, the ASC system proved capable of directing air support for both offensive and defensive operations. Expanded and refined over a period of 12 to 18 months by Air Marshals Tedder, AOC-in-C, RAF Middle East, and Coningham, air officer commanding (AOC), WDAF, a hybrid of the Wann-Woodall system and the air-support experiments in North Africa eventually led to the acceptance of the new joint air-support concepts and the deployment of the revolutionary WDAF system in the summer of 1942.[40]

Another important step along the road to meeting the British Army's air-support requirements was the formation of Army Co-operation Command on 1 December 1940. The Air Staff discussed the creation of such a command in July, but it was a formal request from the army in late September for a new RAF command that "specialised in air support for the Army" that paved the way for its creation. Anthony Eden, the secretary of state for war, reluctantly accepted the necessity of army-RAF co-operation if the air-support problem was to be solved quickly. There was insufficient time (and insufficient resources) for the army to start from scratch and "raise, train, and maintain an Army Air Arm before 1942 at the earliest."[41] The Air Ministry both welcomed and fully supported the War Office's request for a new functional command, similar to Bomber and Fighter Commands, particularly if by meeting this request it could avert at least temporarily another political battle over the RAF's independence. On 18 November, the two services agreed to establish Army Co-operation Command (RAF). Air Marshal Barratt was appointed AOC-in-C, with Woodall, recently promoted to brigadier, serving as his senior air staff officer. The new command was responsible for all air training in co-operation with the army and with the development of the tactics and techniques of Army Co-operation, including close air support. It was successful in improving the technical proficiency of both services when co-operating with each other, but it did not address the larger policy issues concerning command and the optimum use of aircraft in support of land operations.[42]

North Africa: The Adoption and Refinement of a New Air-Land Technique

Harmonious and effective army-RAF co-operation in the Middle East predated the outbreak of the war in the form of the combined plan for the defence of Egypt. British offensive operations against Italian forces in Libya—namely Operation Compass in the autumn of 1940 and Operation Crusader fought during the autumn and winter of 1941–42—also provided irrefutable evidence that integrated planning between air and ground forces worked. Army and air commanders learned firsthand that land and air operations reinforced each other when planned and conducted in the closest consultation. Direct and continuous collaboration familiarised each service with the strengths and the weaknesses of the other. By the spring of 1942, ideas, equipment, and technique merged together and fashioned not only a formidable air weapon to support the army but also led to something entirely new: tactical airpower. Flexible for either attack or defence, the RAF Middle East was organised and trained to fight in equal partnership with land and maritime forces, as well as in its own separate element to command the air above North Africa and over the Mediterranean.[43]

The sine qua non of success in the desert war, indeed of all the major battles and campaigns in the Second World War, was air supremacy. Attainment and retention of air superiority over the battlefield was an essential prerequisite for an effective contribution by air forces to land operations. All other tasks, namely isolating the battlefield from enemy reinforcement and supply, reconnaissance, and attacking targets in forward areas of the contact battle, were secondary until a favourable air situation was established. Air superiority and air support for the land forces were not separate and antipathetic tasks. Once a satisfactory air situation was secured, the whole air force with all of its available strength—if centralised under the direct command and control of the air commander—could be switched to direct support, in effect saturating the battlefield with airpower.[44] These guidelines, simple but sound, were the essence of the Tedder and Coningham doctrine for joint air-land operations.

The process of formulating the new doctrine began during the spring and summer months of 1941. Drawing on recent battle experience and training exercises in the desert, Air Marshal Tedder deduced that the whole North African/Mediterranean campaign was a joint campaign that demanded the utmost interservice co-operation. The co-operation he envisaged involved more than one service drawing up a plan and then approaching the other two services for assistance, which, sadly, was the British Army's historical approach to co-operation. Tedder regarded every operation from its inception as a joint operation that must be planned and executed on that basis. Army and air commanders must work together throughout all stages of drafting, planning, and executing their operations. To this end, he urged both services to maintain intimate contacts at all relevant levels of command, both at their respective permanent headquarters in the Middle East (HQME) and in the field. Such co-operation, he counselled, offered the additional benefit of strengthening the unity of purpose of the services. Tedder firmly believed that integrating both the army and the air force into the larger strategic mission and co-ordinating their actions through a joint plan of operations was the key to victory.[45]

Tedder believed that the best way to win the war in Libya was by combining the unique offensive power of the air force—its flexibility, ubiquity, power of concentration, and ability to penetrate—with the power of the army to contain and occupy. The army would occupy and defend forward landing grounds whilst the air force would strike further afield, thereby assisting the army's forward movement. As such, the fighting services were interdependent. Their success in battle therefore depended in large measure on the degree to which they assisted each other.[46]

Tedder was the thinker who conceived the new air-support system but Air Vice-Marshal Coningham (AOC WDAF) was the practitioner who made it work. Coningham realised that attaining both the flexibility to shift aircraft rapidly from one task to another and the ability to concentrate superior air strength at the decisive time and place were the essential preconditions to turning Tedder's theory into practice. Air forces had to be controlled by one central authority if the maximum value was to be drawn from their unique offensive character. Coningham took the abstract concepts of centralised command and concentration of force and devised the tactical air doctrine that exploited them.[47]

During Operation Crusader, Coningham established his headquarters beside the army commander's. By collocating both air and army staffs and creating a combined army-air headquarters in the field, Coningham was ideally placed to view the battle in its entirety and to take rapid executive action in response to changing circumstances and operational requirements. Coningham commanded what amounted to a unified air force inclusive of all types of bombers, fighters, fighter-bombers, and reconnaissance aircraft, centrally coordinated, in a broad combined plan of employment. Concentrating on battlefield air attack (excluding air transportation and operations by airborne forces), the air forces contributed to land operations in three ways: first by establishing and maintaining air superiority, second by isolating the battlefield, and third by providing direct support for the ground troops.[48]

Coningham's ability to fight an air-land battle was improved considerably by the introduction of two technological innovations: air-support controls and the fighter-bomber (first the Hurribomber and later the Kittyhawk and Tomahawk fighter-bombers). The intricate communications links of the ASCs enabled Coningham to direct and monitor the air battle. Flying from advanced airfields close to the battlefront, fighter-bombers provided air support independently and with a much shorter reaction time than that needed by ordinary bomber and reconnaissance aircraft and their fighter escorts. Fighter-bombers could also revert to their original role as fighters whenever circumstances demanded. Accurate in ground attack and adept at air-to-air combat, the fighter-bomber, as developed by the RAF, was the long-sought-after answer to the German "Stuka" Ju-87 dive-bomber.[49] In tandem the ASCs and the fighter-bombers provided Coningham with a flexible air weapon that enabled the WDAF to seize the tactical initiative.[50]

The WDAF's new air-ground doctrine proved far superior to the German blitzkrieg. During the middle years of the war, both in Russia and North Africa, the Germans increasingly subjugated their air forces to the demands of the ground commander, who wrongly insisted on the provision of close support at the expense of air superiority: the one vital element to sustained offensive initiative now in both air and ground operations.[51] From 1942 through the end of the North African campaign, the

16

WDAF's concept of operations began with the attainment and retention of air superiority. Coningham, more than any other RAF officer, eventually convinced his counterparts in the Eighth Army that air forces could make a decisive contribution to the outcome of a land battle in many ways, the least of which was as flying artillery at the ground force's point of attack. But it was a lengthy and painfully slow process of reeducation.

British generals Sir Claude Auchinleck and Sir Neil Ritchie accepted the basic guidelines of the Tedder and Coningham system, which were codified in March 1942 in the Middle East (army and air) Training Pamphlet No. 3A, *Direct Air Support*.[52] Achieving true coordination between aircraft and forward elements of the army was, however, more problematic. Most ground commanders quite naturally viewed their leading role on the battlefield as a matter of tradition. They were, as Tedder and Coningham discovered, "instinctively antagonistic" to shared operational authority, especially with an airman. They also found it difficult to accept the fact that they did not have "a divine right to command [their] own private air forces."[53] One brigadier even told Coningham that "what a Corps Commander really wants is a squadron at his disposal to come up on his call and bomb something in front of him."[54] His candid comment betrayed a deeply rooted bias about aircraft serving as nothing more than auxiliary weapons for the army: one he shared with many other corps, division, and brigade commanders. More than any other obstacle, it was the lack of conceptual commonality—strategic, operational, and tactical—between soldiers and airmen that was the most difficult problem to overcome. It was the harsh test of battle that exposed the flaws and identified the solutions.

Rommel's 1942 spring offensive against the Gazala positions began with brilliant success on 26 May and ended in stalemate 42 days later at El Alamein, some 220 miles inside the Egyptian border.[55] A rough comparison of the opposing numbers of tanks and aircraft reveals that the British had a substantial numerical advantage on the ground whilst the Germans had a similar edge in the air. Lack of air support for the army was not, however, the reason for the Eighth Army's failure, a point fully accepted by General Auchinleck: "Our air forces could not have done more than they did to help and sustain the 8th Army in its struggle. Their effort was continuous by day and by night and the effect on the enemy was tremendous. . . . Had it not been for their devoted and exceptional efforts, we should not have been able to stop the enemy on the El Alamein position."[56] Enemy war diaries corroborate General Auckinleck's assessment.[57] The problem, such as it was for the British in the Middle East, was the systemic weaknesses of the army in the field.[58]

Tedder was incensed at the army's defeatist attitude and its poorly coordinated response to the German offensive. He did not doubt either the bravery or the courage of the British soldier, but he harboured serious misgivings about the lack of leadership exhibited by the army's senior officers.[59] The inherent weaknesses in the army's organisation were exacerbated by the confusion and strain of the retreat: a pernicious combination unlikely to improve the performance of the fledgling army-air co-operation system. Under enemy pressure the Eighth Army—retreating all too often in headlong panic—demonstrated a fundamental disregard for the air-support arrangements that had been agreed on with the WDAF. Coningham was obliged to rely almost entirely on his own tactical reconnaissance in order to give the army any support at all.[60] Auchinleck empathised with Coningham's legitimate grievances, but he seemed powerless to rectify the situation.[61]

Effective co-operation, as the historian John Terraine has stated, depends entirely on how well all the parties involved work together: "The system fails if one party to it collapses, which is what the Eighth Army too frequently did in the face of the Afrika Korps."[62] The WDAF could not be expected on its own to produce the desired victory. Nevertheless, it was instrumental in preventing a catastrophic defeat.

The combined German and Italian armies reached the British positions at El Alamein at the end of June. Rommel commenced his attack on 1 July. Soon after, it was a decision he regretted bitterly. Co-operation from air forces was of decisive importance in a land battle at this stage in the war, and the first battle of El Alamein provided a stark illustration of this point.[63]

The Luftwaffe was exhausted, and without air support Rommel's Panzerarmee could not dislodge the Eighth Army from its defensive positions; meanwhile the Axis ground troops were subjected to a powerful and punishing air assault. During the first week of July alone, the WDAF flew 5,458 sorties against Rommel's forces. As was the case during the latter stages of the Eighth Army's retreat into Egypt, Coningham fought an independent air battle, selecting targets on the basis of his own reconnaissance. Auchinleck, despite his genuine belief in the importance of air support, maintained a separate army headquarters throughout the battle. Whilst the joint system, so carefully devised over the previous nine months, clearly had broken down, the overwhelming might of Allied airpower under the dual leadership of Tedder and Coningham proved too much for the overextended Afrika Korps. On 4 July, Rommel informed Berlin that he was suspending the offensive and taking up defensive positions.[64]

During the stalemate that followed, both sides struggled to build up their forces for the next and possibly final battle. HQME also used the lull in the fighting to deduce the lessons of the recent debacle. At an army commanders' meeting on 16 July, Tedder was questioned about the RAF's supposed failure to provide close support. He responded with a detailed account of the WDAF's recent accomplishments, noting that without it the army's retreat "would have become a shambles." Effective direct support, Tedder restated, depended on both services helping each other. Too often this was not the case. The WDAF was forced to collect its own information on the battle, and it seldom received adequate bomb lines from the troops it was tasked to support. Unimpressed with this explanation, a couple of generals confronted Tedder after the meeting and said "it was about time there was some plain speaking on the subject." Tedder could not have agreed more, but he also noted that "to try and make an impression on the Army was rather like hitting a wall of cotton wool."[65]

By early August, the army's senior commanders in the Middle East had lost the confidence of the prime minister and the War Cabinet in London. Auckinleck was sacked. Gen Sir Harold Alexander took his place as the theatre commander, and General Montgomery was appointed commander of the Eighth Army.[66]

Montgomery brought to the Eighth Army an immediate and infectious winning attitude. His first order, issued on 13 August, two days prior to taking up command, was that the army forthwith would hold its ground. Instantly, Montgomery instilled a sense of purpose and direction in the army, something that had been absent for far too long. "Orders no longer formed 'the basis for discussion' but for action." Montgomery firmly believed that "command must be direct and personal." He also believed that a commander must plan his operations thoroughly in advance.[67]

The WDAF also felt Montgomery's presence with advantage. Coningham met Montgomery on 16 August. The two men soon discovered that they held similar views on the benefits of a commander exercising personal control over his forces in battle. They talked about the importance of air superiority as a prerequisite for both effective air support and victory in a land battle, and also about the merits of a joint command system. Montgomery listened, and before their meeting ended he pledged to move his headquarters immediately in order to be beside Coningham. Montgomery was even better than his word. The advanced HQs of both services were not only collocated, but they joined together and remained this way for the duration of the campaign. It was an auspicious day for the Allies. Montgomery did what no previous British general in the desert had been willing to do: he worked out his plans and fought his battles together with the air force.[68]

There was "a spirit of quiet confidence" at the joint Army Air Headquarters.[69] Together Montgomery and Coningham had worked out a joint plan to coordinate and direct their impending operations. Comprehensive victories in the Battle of Alam el Halfa and the Second Battle of El Alamein attest to the effectiveness of their partnership and the merits of the new air-support system. Afterwards, a despondent Rommel wrote that "anyone who has to fight against an enemy with air superiority fights under the same handicaps and with the same chances of success as a savage against modern European troops."[70] The success achieved is correctly attributed to the system devised by Tedder and Coningham, but the system alone was not antecedent to successful operations. Continuous and intimate collaboration between Coningham and Montgomery accounts for the triumphant application of airpower. The personalities involved were as instrumental to the success attained as the new procedures themselves. Force of personality also led to the ac-

20

ceptance of a new doctrine. From the Battle of Alam el Halfa to the victorious end of the campaign at Tunis in May 1943, the air-support system established by Tedder and Coningham was accepted and implemented by the Eighth Army. Air superiority was the key to success, and attaining it received priority.[71]

Under Montgomery the army accepted the fact that direct support was only a part, and often a small part, of the critical support provided by air forces during a land battle. Sadly, this was not the case with the Operation Torch landings and the early Anglo-American operations in Northwest Africa.

Operation Torch was the first major attempt the American and British allies made at joint and combined operations. General Eisenhower was the commander in chief. His task-force commander was British lieutenant-general K. A. N. Anderson. An overall air commander did not figure in the Torch plan. British and American air forces were to operate separately and in different geographical areas.[72] No provisions were made for liaison between the two air forces, and they formed their plans without reference to each other. In addition to the rigid demarcation lines for operations, which negated the RAF's first principles of air-power—namely concentration of force and flexibility of action—the Torch planners gave army and corps commanders clear operational control over their supporting air forces.[73] In Northwest Africa the air forces were subordinate to the land forces.

The Torch planners, later to their regret, ignored the hard-earned lessons learnt by the RAF in the Middle East. Neither the Tedder/Coningham command system nor the combat-proven procedures and techniques of the WDAF were taken into account. Instead the Anglo-American air planners looked to an untried American doctrine, outlined in Field Manual (FM) 31-35, *Aviation in Support of Ground Forces*, for their air-ground policy. On paper it offered a comprehensive tactical air control system: a central air command, a sophisticated network of ASC centres, and various levels of communications between the ground and the air forces. In practice, the techniques had yet to be developed. FM 31-35's emphasis on corps-level air support also was inclined to foster the dispersion and subordination of the air force to the narrow close-support interests of the ground commanders. All other air operations, which often were more important to the outcome of a land campaign, were left unattended. It was, as one historian, Richard Hallion, has concluded, "the kind of system the British Army wanted in 1939–1941."[74] Terraine blames Air Marshal Sir Charles Portal, chief of the Air Staff, and the Air Staff for allowing these "inexcusable" shortcomings in air-support doctrine and planning to go forward. Others, however, rightly point out that burgeoning American influence, in particular that of Generals Eisenhower and Carl Spaatz, was responsible for the Torch air plan.[75]

Both in concept and in execution, the air support provided for Operation Torch was woefully inadequate. Bombers and fighters were kept "on call" by senior army commanders who insisted on receiving continuous protection from enemy air attack and on having aircraft immediately available for local ground-assault tasks.[76] British and American air commanders were quick to criticise this "improper employment" of their forces. But their remonstrations fell on deaf ears. A wider application of airpower—to establish air superiority, isolate the battle area, and disrupt the enemy's communications and supplies—seemed to be well beyond the experience and the limited understanding of the soldiers. In the words of one American fighter-group leader, "The army generals did not care two hoots about air superiority."[77] Furthermore, the gross misuse of Allied airpower in Northwest Africa enabled the numerically inferior Luftwaffe to secure local air superiority and successfully attack Anglo-American ground troops on a frequent basis. Less than a month after the Allied landings, the advance on Tunisia had slowed to a virtual halt. Eisenhower was learning the hard way that victory on the ground depended in large measure on the effective employment of airpower.

Help arrived at the end of November when Tedder visited Eisenhower's headquarters in Algiers. The two commanders enjoyed a number of candid discussions on the growing crisis in air support and the many difficulties revealed in the Torch setup. Tedder was "deeply disturbed" by what he saw and heard.[78] In addition to the tactical heresy committed by the ground commanders, he observed that communications for all of the services were practically nonexistent, landing grounds were wholly inadequate in both number and location (the most advanced fighter airfield was more than 100 miles behind the forward troops), and there was not even the semblance of a joint headquarters to control air operations.[79] Altogether these shortcomings negated the possibility of achieving a high standard of concentrated air effort and hence air superiority.[80] These were familiar problems. Their remedy, also found in the recent past, depended on a complete reorganisation of the control of air operations.

Effective and efficient air support was, for Tedder, contingent on proper organisation and centralised control. It was a problem of executive decision making as much as or even more than one of tactical coordination and execution in the field. In Northwest Africa, the problem was complicated further by the political considerations of coalition warfare. This last hurdle was the most crucial one because, in Tedder's opinion, the solution was a unified Anglo-American air force under a single air command with operational responsibility for all of North Africa and the Mediterranean. Only the RAF had the experience and the expertise to create and run such a command. Moreover, American acceptance of British ideas and procedures was by no means certain. Tedder knew this. He also knew that endorsement of his proposal required both careful management and tact. After a series of preliminary discussions involving Eisenhower, Tedder, Portal, and the chiefs of staff (COS) in London, the COSs, on 1 December 1942, proposed that all of the Torch air forces be integrated under Tedder's command. In his capacity as AOC-in-C, he would also serve as Eisenhower's air adviser.[81]

Eisenhower had some reservations, but in general he agreed with the recommendation for a unified command system. The radical nature of the proposed changes meant that numerous practical details had to be resolved before anything could actually be implemented. Not until the Casablanca Conference in mid-January 1943, in the presence of Pres. Franklin D. Roosevelt, Churchill, and the combined (British and American) COSs, were all of the various arrangements finalised. Even then it was not until 17 February that Tedder's appointment as AOC-in-C, Mediterranean, took effect, and the Northwest African Air Forces (NWAAF) was constituted. Eastern Air Command and the Twelfth US Army Air Force combined to form the NWAAF under the command of General Spaatz.[82] The Americans also accepted the RAF concept of dividing air operations by function rather than by geographic zones. The NWAAF was subdivided into

23

the Northwest African Strategic Air Force under Gen James "Jimmy" Doolittle, the Northwest African Coastal Air Force under Air Vice-Marshal Sir Hugh Pugh Lloyd, and the newly created Northwest African Tactical Air Force (NATAF) under Marshal Coningham.[83]

The debacle at Kasserine, which coincidently occurred at the same time that the Allied air forces were reconstituted, led to further and even more radical changes in American air doctrine.[84] Coningham arrived at the front on 18 February and immediately changed the air-support arrangements. He discontinued American methods (prescribed in FM 31-35) and replaced them with his own WDAF organisation and system of command. Centralised control was the fundamental premise. Coningham therefore assumed direct command of all tactical air units (No. 242 Group, RAF, and XII Air Support Command, US Army Air Forces) and ended the flawed and harmful practice of land commanders controlling aircraft. Corps and division commanders now made their requests for air support through the highest army commander (Gen Sir Harold Alexander, C-in-C 18th Army Group), who shared a joint headquarters with Coningham and his air staff. Communications, as in Egypt and Cyrenaica, were handled through an ASC network.[85]

On 20 February, Coningham issued his first general operational directive to NATAF. He emphasised that the first priority was the establishment of air superiority, and second was the isolation of the immediate battlefield. Henceforth, air support would be proactive and offensive. The practice of standing fighter patrols (air umbrellas) to protect friendly ground troops was replaced by offensive fighter sweeps against the enemy air force at or near its bases. Ground attack missions would also focus on targets in the rearward areas, namely troop concentrations and columns of soft-skinned vehicles, rather than tanks and enemy troops deployed at the battlefront. Close support (the American term), or direct support of ground forces, became a minor duty of the air forces. Its decline in importance was not, however, a rejection of the army's needs; rather it was a prudent shift in accordance with established and battle-proven RAF doctrine. Except for the Battle of El Hamma, from 3 to 9 April, when the NATAF flew more than 3,000 sorties and dropped over 1,500,000 pounds of bombs in direct support of the forward elements of the army, the campaign in Northwest Africa did not lend itself to major close-support operations.[86]

To their considerable credit, American commanders accepted Coningham's idea of independent air support. During the spring of 1943, Eisenhower established a study group to examine the lessons of Kasserine and to make recommendations for a new field manual to replace FM 31-35. He also sent his air operations officer, Brig Gen Lawrence S. Kuter, back to Washington to promote the new air-ground relationship. Air Force generals Henry H. "Hap" Arnold and Spaatz were equally enthusiastic about the British concepts, and in July 1943 the US Army published FM 100-20, *Command and Employment of Air Power*. It specified three phases of an air campaign in support of a land operation and listed them in order of priority: "to gain and maintain air superiority, to isolate the battlefield, and to support the ground forces."[87] In short, the Americans adopted the British doctrine in toto.[88] What the British Army had failed to do after three and a half years of war, the Americans did in less than nine months. They not only proclaimed airpower and land power equal and interdependent—neither being an auxiliary of the other—but also accepted them as such. In future land campaigns, control of all available airpower would be exercised through the air force commander, who would work with rather than for the land commander.[89] In the arid wastes of North Africa, Allied air and ground commanders working together learned the art of joint operations and thereby found the key that opened the door to victory.

Success without Harmony: British Air-Land Co-operation by the End of the War

Montgomery grasped both the essential character and the importance of air operations in support of a land battle. In the Western Desert he worked closely with Coningham at all stages of drafting, planning, and executing integrated air-ground operations. Success in battle depended on the degree to which the army and the air force assisted each other, not as ancillary to the other but as equals in pursuit of a common objective. Both men also benefited from Tedder's strategic vision. Tedder viewed war "as a single problem in which the strategy, and tactics, and the technique of sea, land and air warfare respectively are inevitably and closely interlocked."[90] Together, Montgomery and Coningham turned Tedder's theory into battlefield practice, achieved a high degree of co-operation, and created a winning air-land combination on the desert battlefields in North Africa. Montgomery's monumental ego eventually came to the fore and sabotaged his relationship with Coningham and other British and American commanders, but it was that same ego and burning desire to defeat the Germans that led him to search out his air counterpart and construct a winning strategy in the summer of 1942.[91]

The debate over the future of army-air co-operation in the UK had not moved on much since the winter of 1940–41. The army still wanted its own air arm under its direct command and control, and the RAF still refused to countenance such an extravagant and unsound use of finite air resources. Drawing on the recent lessons of army-air co-operation in North Africa, Marshal Portal told his army counterpart in May 1943 that the RAF would provide air support for Operation Overlord (and the subsequent Normandy campaign), along the lines of the WDAF system.[92] Portal's proposal did not meet with the War Office's approval. In particular, Gen Alan Brooke, chief of the Imperial General Staff, still held out for the creation of an independent army-air arm. The deadlock was eventually broken by a combination of factors: the battlefield success achieved by Montgomery and Coningham in the Western Desert from August 1942 onwards; Churchill's personal intervention in October 1942 when he restated the terms of the Middle East Directive on Air Support for the benefit of the army and the RAF in the United Kingdom; Fighter Command's development of air-support techniques; and Exercise Spartan, the last of the great Home Forces exercises, which ran for 12 days, from 1 to 12 March 1943, and illustrated the clear advantages of a unified air force under centralised control over all other methods of meeting the army's air-support needs.[93] Reluctantly, Brooke and the General Staff acquiesced under the insurmountable pressure and accepted the Air Staff's methods for providing air support. A victory of intellect and procedure had been achieved, but it had taken an inordinate amount of effort and was secured at considerable cost both in time and lives lost.

With the formation of the Second Tactical Air Force (TAF) on 1 June 1943, a policy that the RAF and the army had agreed upon as the most effective and efficient means of providing air support for the British armies in the field had been achieved.[94] From this point in the war to its end, the army received substantial air support in its battles against the enemy. As for the RAF, its independence and first principles had been preserved, and its concept of air warfare in support of land forces was both accepted and practised. This marked a significant departure, though not, sadly, the end of a long and tortuous dispute between the two services dating back to the last years of the First World War. At its heart were vexing differences over the essential character of air warfare and a bitter struggle over who would manage limited air forces during a war and how. These appear to be innate problems and ones that the Anglo-American armies and air forces of the latter stages of the Second World War successfully managed rather than solved.

Back to Afghanistan and Contemporary Air-Land Integration

RAF historian Sir Maurice Dean identified three fundamental features of effective army-air co-operation: the willingness to co-operate (goodwill), sound principles and tactics, and reliable communications.[95] By the summer of 1942 all three were in evidence in the British Army and the Western Desert Air Force (RAF) as they fought a series of successful joint battles in North Africa. These basic requirements, according to Wing Cdr Harv Smyth (RAF), appear to have been forgotten by the British Army and the RAF in the early years of the twenty-first century and had to be relearned after Operation Telic, the UK's contribution to Operation Iraqi Freedom, the war to liberate Iraq fought between 20 March and 22 April 2003. Smyth expanded Dean's list of key characteristics for successful air-land integration, citing five factors, which he divided into two groups: "key enablers" and "specific to the implementation of air-land operations." His enablers include "air superiority and centralised command of air support assets." His three factors specific to the suc-

27

cessful conduct of air-land operations are "command and control (C2) structures, training and doctrine, and tactical level situational awareness."[96] Through his comparative analysis of both the 1942 North Africa Campaign and Operation Telic, Smyth concludes that British forces did indeed have to relearn historical air-land lessons but only relearned those that were in his group of enablers—air superiority and the need for centralised (air) command and control. What were not achieved by either the 1942 British Army and RAF in North Africa or British forces fighting in Iraq in 2003, according to Smyth, were the essential skill sets and structures that are the specific prerequisites for effective and successfully conducted air-land operations. Smyth further states that during Telic "the British implementation of Close Air Support (CAS) was most lacking."[97]

It is highly unlikely that Major Loden and his men, fighting in Helmand Province during the summer of 2006, would have disagreed with Smyth's criticism of the RAF's ability to deliver effective close air support. Twice during intense close-contact battles with Taliban forces, Loden's unit received "support" from RAF Harriers. Both times the results were much less than helpful. On one occasion, Loden states that "a female Harrier pilot couldn't identify the target, fired 2 phosphorous rockets that just missed our own compound so that we thought they were incoming RPGs [rocket-propelled grenades], and then strafed our perimeter missing the enemy by 200 metres." On the second occasion, Loden was with his fire-support team as it tried to coordinate air support against Taliban guerrillas, which were deploying heavy weapons from positions in-depth against a British infantry assault consisting of two platoons and numbering some 80 men. "We began to engage them with mortars," Loden recorded. "Once more the RAF Harriers overhead could not identify a target, but would have been too close anyway for bombs. Nonetheless they fired a rocket that missed by about 700 metres. Thankfully by this stage 2 Apaches arrived." Loden's fire-support team successfully directed the Apache attack helicopters onto a number of enemy positions, which were silenced by accurate direct fire.[98]

Enduring Themes and
Contemporary Relevance

Loden's frustration with the RAF Harriers that were meant to provide him with air support is understandable even if his detailed criticisms are not always accurate. RAF Harriers do not carry guns, so the female pilot who supposedly strafed Loden and his men either was not flying a Harrier or, at the very least, did not strafe them. Nonetheless, Loden's command did suffer a number of casualties, and he, like many army commanders both now on current operations and those who have fought in the battles of a more distant past, harbours a searing belief that ineffective air support was to blame for the deaths and setbacks his unit suffered. Yet despite his bitterness, when Loden reflected on his battles against the Taliban in August 2006, he came to the same conclusion that General Montgomery reached more than 60 years earlier in the Western Desert. Loden was of the firm belief that his experience "proves once again the old lesson, that all arms and services must be fit and capable" and they must work together.[99] To achieve effective air-land coordination on the battlefield in Afghanistan, as was the case in North Africa during the Second World War, requires the services, as equal partners, to work together toward a common plan aimed at achieving common objectives.

British efforts to improve air-land integration began in 2003 with Project Coningham-Keyes (PC-K), well before the army and the RAF began to experience problems fighting together in Helmand Province. PC-K is a two-star led, triservice undertaking to identify the air-land lessons from Operation Telic. Three separate working groups, each one led by one of the services, have been tasked to investigate a discrete set of doctrinal, operational, technological, and joint training issues, all of which have been deemed essential for the development of a more capable and robust British air-support system. Land Command is responsible for concepts and C2; Fleet has the lead in battlespace and intelligence, surveillance, target acquisition, and reconnaissance; and Air is in charge of training and simulation. The three groups have focused their efforts mainly on fundamental issues at the operational and tactical levels, and a number of positive developments have resulted from this ongoing investigation. For example, the creation of the Joint Air/Land Organisation (JALO) has centralised the development of air-land integration. Technological solutions for future air support, new doctrine, and relevant training for the air and land forces all fall under the JALO's broad remit to identify and disseminate best practices in air-land integration. The JALO also acts as a bridge between frontline command and the recommendations that continue to flow out of the successful work produced by Project Coningham-Keyes.[100]

In addition to the tactical and technical initiatives of PC-K, the Royal Air Force Centre for Air Power Studies, the director of defence studies, and King's College London have taken the lead in organising a series of more conceptual studies to identify the problems and recommend solutions to the air-support dilemma. Some of these initiatives have been in direct response to Loden's public criticisms, which also ensured the attention of the service chiefs. With the chiefs' endorsement, a number of air-land conferences and seminars have been held at the Air Warfare Centre in Lincolnshire and at both the Joint Services Command and Staff College and the UK Defence Academy in Shrivenham, Oxfordshire. These conferences and study groups have varied in format, with some being open to a wider academic and military audience and others restricted to British armed forces personnel only. Additional academic/historical input has come from the RAF's Air Historical Branch (AHB) as well as the Naval Historical Branch. In the spring of 2007, the head of the AHB, RAF led a three-star level staff ride to Normandy. "Applied history," studied in the outdoor classroom, enabled senior army and air force commanders to explore contemporary air-land integration issues through their examination of Anglo-American army-air co-operation in the Normandy Campaign.[101] Taken all together, these investigative/scholarly initiatives have not only put air-land operations on centre stage, they have enhanced the acceptance of a more common language between Britain's soldiers and airmen, and helped both achieve a far better understanding of the problems and the possible solutions to achieving more effective air-land integration for the British armed forces.

Improved air-land integration, however, is only going to happen if both soldiers and airmen work together. As one air marshal stated recently: "It is not rocket science, but it needs a collective will to make it so." In some respects, there is nothing new here—whether it was the Battle of Amiens in 1918, the British retreat from Tobruk in 1942, or Operation Granby (the British contribution to Gulf War I, the liberation of Kuwait, 1990–91)—the reasons behind the failure to achieve effective air-land integration are all too similar. Soldiers and airmen have not worked together on a common plan, and they have lacked an essential understanding of the operating requirements of the other's service. When they have made an attempt to understand each other and co-operate fully, as Montgomery and Coningham did in the summer of 1942, the end results have been very positive. In fairness, the RAF has done better at trying to bridge the conceptual gaps between the two services than the army. On a recent Higher Command and Staff College (HCSC) "staff ride," a highly decorated colonel, destined for quick promotion to brigadier and command of one of the army's brigades, was insufferably dismissive of the whole concept of air-land integration. "I am bored with all of this air cooperation," he said. "What I, an army commander, want is to call up air when I need it to bomb something in front of me."[102] Oh, if only it were this simple.

Effective air-land integration requires both soldiers and airmen to give it equal attention and importance in their respective planning and training programmes. Air and land forces need to train together. Training planning echoes that of live operations planning, and it must be undertaken as a joint action, each service being coequal with the other. Churchill said as much in his 5 September 1941 directive to the army and air force commanders in chief, Middle East, when he declared that "co-operation was to come from a combined [joint] plan of action drafted by the services working together as equals. Unity of purpose would be their guide . . . to achieve a common objective."[103] The concepts of "supporting" and "supported" are therefore dated and inappropriate, and they merely confirm the legacy of the dysfunctional command relationship that existed between the army and the RFC in France during the First World War, with air being an ancillary arm to the army. Just as the German army and air force found a force multiplier in the way they combined armour with aircraft in their highly successful blitzkrieg tactics of 1940, Britain's land and air commanders today must believe that working together is the right thing to do. A combination of better co-ordination of training, greater personal interaction between the army and the RAF at all levels, and a much better understanding of each service's common and uncommon characteristics will all enhance the delivery of better air-land integration.[104] It is a massive challenge, but then, what is the alternative if this opportunity is lost?

Notes

1. Operation Herrick is the code name under which all British operations in Afghanistan have been conducted since 2002. Herrick IV is the name given to the operations conducted between May and November 2006.

2. Wing Cdr Ian Duguid as quoted by BBC News, "RAF Afghanistan Footage Released," 4 October 2006, 19:50 GMT. See http://news.bbc.co.uk/go/pr/fr/-/1/hi/world/south_asia/5408086.stm.

3. Maj James Loden, commander, Company A, 3 PARA, "E-mails from Helmand," edited for circulation, *Guardian*, 23 September 2006. See Mark Townsend, "RAF Retaliates over Useless Jibes," *Observer* (London), 24 September 2006, 3; Kim Sengupta, "Army Chief Leaps to Defence of UK's Afghan Mission; Leaked Complaints from Frontline Officers Fighting in Helmand Are 'Irresponsible,'" *Independent on Sunday* (London), 2nd ed., 24 September 2006, 4; and Alan Cowell, "British Army Rejects Complaints from Officers," *International Herald Tribune* (Paris), 3rd ed., 25 September 2006, 3. For an account of 3 PARA's operations in Afghanistan during the summer of 2006, see Patrick Bishop, *3 PARA: Afghanistan, Summer 2006. This is War* (London: HarperPress, 2007).

4. The Directorate of Operational Capability has been conducting an audit into air-land integration since May 2007 and is due to send its report to the vice-chief of the defense staff and the chief of staff (COS) for final endorsement before the end of the summer 2008. In addition to this report, Project Coningham-Keyes, a triservice, two-star led investigation into British air support following Operation Telic, is in the second stage of its enquiry.

5. "Memorandum on the Co-operation of Air Forces with the BEF [British Expeditionary Force]," 18 June 1940, The National Archives (TNA) of the United Kingdom, War Office (WO) 106/1754; and WO (MO7) memorandum by Lt Col F. W. Festing, "Direct Support of the BEF in France," June 1940, TNA AIR [reference code for Air Ministry, RAF] 20/4447.

6. Brig C. Greenslade, DQMC, BEF, "Report on the Operations of the British Expeditionary Force," 17 June 1940, TNA WO 197/111.

7. Air Marshal Douglas as quoted in "Army/Air Co-operation," C. E. Carrington Papers, 81/11/6, Imperial War Museum, London.

8. See David Ian Hall, *Strategy for Victory: The Development of British Tactical Air Power, 1919–1943* (Westport, CT: Praeger Security International, 2008).

9. See B. Michael Bechthold, "A Question of Success: Tactical Practice in North Africa, 1942–43," *Journal of Military History* 68, no. 3 (July 2004): 821–51; Paul Johnston, "The Question of British Influence on US Tactical Air Power in World War II," *Air Power History* 52, no.1 (Spring 2005); and David R. Mets, "A Glider in the Propwash of the RAF," in *Air Power and Ground Armies: Essays on the Evolution of Anglo-American Air Doctrine, 1940–1943*, ed. Daniel R. Mortensen (Maxwell AFB, AL: Air University Press, 1998), 45–91.

10. Gen Sir William Nicholson, CIGS, War Office communiqué to the press, 23 July 1908, reprinted in C. F. Snowden Gamble, *The Air Weapon* (Oxford: Oxford University Press, 1931), 109–10. See also Alfred Gollin, *The Impact of Air Power on the British People and Their Government, 1909–1914* (Basingstoke, UK: Macmillan, 1989), 11–12.

11. The list of such senior army officers is depressingly long. Some of the more prominent antagonists include Generals Sir Henry Maitland "Jumbo" Wilson, John Gort, Edmund Ironside, Sir John Dill, Sir William Bartholomew, and Alan Brooke, and Lt Col F. W. Festing (the head of MO7, the War Office department responsible for Army-Air Co-operation, established in January 1940, and consisting of Festing and three other Army officers).

12. Three of the more prominent early advocates of the aeroplane and military aeronautics were Winston Churchill, Capt George Sandys (the conservative member of parliament for the Wells Division of Somerset), and Col J. E. B. Seely. See Gollin, *Impact of Air Power*, 180–85.

13. For a complete list of the membership of this committee, see ibid., 185. For a short account of the early years of service aviation in Britain see Malcolm Cooper, *The Birth of Independent Air Power* (London: Allen and Unwin, 1986), 1–12. See also Sir Walter Raleigh and H. A. Jones, *The War in the Air*, vol. 1 (Oxford: The Clarendon Press, 1922), chaps. 4 and 5.

14. *Report of the Technical Standing Sub-Committee of the Committee of Imperial Defence on Aerial Navigation*, 28 February 1912, TNA CAB [reference code for Cabinet] 38/20/1; Minutes of the 116th meeting of the CID, 25 April 1912, TNA CAB 38/20/9; WO memorandum, "Naval and Military Aviation," 11 April 1912, as quoted in "Foundation of British Air Service" (lecture 12 in series "Role of the RAF in War"), Trenchard Papers, MFC 76/1/357, RAF Museum, RAF Hendon, London.

15. Cooper, *Birth of Independent Air Power*, 9. When the war began, the RNAS had 100 aircraft (of which half were serviceable) and one airship.

16. At the end of the First World War, the RAF mustered almost 300,000 personnel and some 22,000 aircraft (ibid., xv).

17. For a comprehensive account of the evolution of military aviation during the Great War (1914–18), see S. F. Wise, *Canadian Airmen and the First World War: The Official History of the Royal Canadian Air Force*, vol. 1 (Toronto: University of Toronto Press, 1980); W. Sholto Douglas, *Years of Combat: A Personal Story of the First World War in the Air* (London: Collins, 1963); and Denis Winter, *The First of the Few: Fighter Pilots of the First World War* (London: Allen Lane, 1982).

18. Lee Kennett, "Developments to 1939," in *Case Studies in the Development of Close Air Support*, ed. B. F. Cooling (Washington, DC: Office of Air

Force History, US Air Force, 1990), 17–23; and Peter C. Smith, *Close Air Support* (Shrewsbury: Airlife, 1990), 8.

19. "Foundation of British Air Service" (lecture 12), 2–3, Trenchard Papers, MFC 76/1/357.

20. Shelford Bidwell and Dominick Graham, *Fire Power* (London: George Allen and Unwin, 1982), 20–21; J. C. Slessor, *Air Power and Armies* (Oxford: Oxford University Press, 1936), 87–88; and Kennett, "Developments to 1939," 15–16.

21. Increasing demands for large numbers of aircraft from 1916 onwards, and the difficulties encountered in producing them, gave rise to acute differences between the Admiralty and the War Office over the direction of Britain's air effort. As each service struggled to obtain its own separate and highly specialised air support, the wider development of a comprehensive air policy suffered. During the summer of 1917, daylight raids on London by German "Gotha" bombers brought the whole unhappy history of interservice cooperation on air matters to the attention of the general public and the politicians alike. In response to the shock of Germany's aerial bombardment of London, the government took action to improve the confused state of administration and organisation of Britain's air forces. Acting on the recommendations made in a report written by Gen Jan Christian Smuts, the British government established a single independent air service with its own ministry and air staff, which was responsible for all aspects of war in the air. The RAF was created on 1 April 1918, and it was given a broad mandate to pursue the strategic and operational roles of British air forces in war. See Cooper, *Birth of Independent Air Power*, 42–70, 97–107; Sir Charles Webster and Noble Frankland, *The Strategic Air Offensive against Germany, 1939–1945* (London, Her Majesty's Stationery Office [HMSO], 1961), 36–37; and "Policy 1917–1923" (lecture 1), 1–2, Trenchard Papers, MFC 76/1/357. For the entire text of Smuts's second report, *The Second Report of the Prime Minister's Committee on the Air Organisation and Home Defence against Air Raids*, 17 August 1917, see Raleigh and Jones, *War in the Air*, appendices 8–14.

22. Slessor, *Air Power and Armies*, passim; see also J. P. Harris and Niall Barr, *Amiens to the Armistice: The BEF in the Hundred Days' Campaign, 8 August–11 November 1918* (London: Brassey's, 1998).

23. The British Army did not produce an official report on the lessons of the Great War until 1932, and even then this report was not published until 1934. See "Lessons of the 1914–1918 War," 1932, TNA WO 32/3115; and Gen W. Kirke, "Report on the Lessons of the Great War," 1934, TNA WO 32/3116.

24. TNA AIR 5/299. The RAF's first official attempt to codify the lessons of the 1914–1918 war in the form of an air doctrine began in 1922 with the publication of RAF Operations Manual CD 22 (sometimes referred to as Air Publication [AP] 882, later reissued with revisions in 1928 as the *RAF War Manual Part I—Operations*, AP 1300).

25. "Some Personal Reflections by MRAF [Marshal of the RAF] Sir John Slessor," September 1964, Liddell Hart Papers 1/644, Liddell Hart Centre for Military Archives, King's College, London.

26. Sir Maurice Dean, *The Royal Air Force and Two World Wars* (London: Cassell, 1979), 34.

27. Remarks by the chief of the Air Staff (Lord Trenchard), 30 May 1921, TNA AIR 8/2.

28. David Ian Hall, "Ruling the Empire out of the Central Blue," *Air Power Review* 10, no. 2 (Summer 2007): 68–76; and RAF AP 3003, *A Brief History of the Royal Air Force* (Norwich: HMSO, 2004), 49–69. See also David E. Omissi, *Air Power and Colonial Control* (Manchester: Manchester University Press, 1990).

29. Derek J. P. Waldie, "Relations between the Army and the Royal Air Force, 1918–1939" (PhD thesis, King's College, London, 1980), 296.

30. Hall, *Strategy for Victory*, 22–24.

31. The AASF, under the operational command of Air Vice-Marshal P. H. L. Playfair, and equipped with 10 squadrons of Fairey Battles, was conceived as a temporary outpost of Bomber Command based in France. Only in extreme circumstances would it be diverted from strategic targets to provide support for the army. The air component, under the command of Air Vice-Marshal C. H. Blount, was a mixed force of four squadrons of fighters, four squadrons of bombers, and four squadrons of army co-operation/reconnaissance aircraft. It was to provide direct air support for the BEF and was under the operational control of General Gort, commander in chief (C-in-C) BEF. See Hall, *Strategy for Victory*, 41–43.

32. WO note, "Arrangements for Bomber Support for the Allied Army in France,"16 November 1939, TNA WO 106/1597.

33. "Operations in France, September 1939–June 1940," Evill Papers, archive collection (AC) 74/8, RAF Museum, RAF Hendon, London; "Army Air Support," 14, TNA WO 277; and RAF AP 3235, *Air Support* (Air Ministry, 1955), 14, TNA AIR 10/5547.

34. RAF figures put the number of combat-ready aircraft in Britain at the start of May 1940 at 692 aircraft, a total that includes both bombers and fighters. RAF AP 3235, *Air Support*, 20.

35. "Air Staff Note on the Army Air Arm," July 1940, TNA AIR 20/3706; and Group Capt R. V. Goddard, D. D. Plans (MC), "Air Ministry Note on the War Office Point of View Regarding Close Support," 22 July 1940, TNA WO 106/5161.

36. See David Ian Hall, "Lessons not Learned: The Struggle between the Royal Air Force and Army for the Tactical Control of Aircraft, and the Postmortem on the Defeat of the British Expeditionary Force in France in 1940," in *The Challenges of High Command: The British Experience*, eds. Gary Sheffield and Geoffrey Till (Basingstoke: Palgrave Macmillan, 2003), 113–25.

37. TNA CAB 65/7 WM 157(40)2, 7 June 1940; and Bartholomew Committee, "Lessons to be Learnt from Operations in Flanders," final report, June 1940, TNA CAB 106/220.

38. Air Vice-Marshal C. H. R. Blount, AOC RAF Component, BEF, was the only airman interviewed. Bartholomew Committee, "Lessons to be Learnt," TNA CAB 106/220.

39. Wann-Woodall Report, "Statement of the Objective of the Trials." Copies of this report, along with critical notes, are contained in "Close Support by Bomber and Fighter Aircraft," TNA AIR 39/140. See also "Army Air Requirements," TNA WO 106/5161; and "Proposed Establishment of Close Support Bomber Control," TNA WO 106/5162.

40. John Terraine, foreword in Charles Carrington, *Soldier at Bomber Command* (London: Leo Cooper, 1987), x. See also Hall, *Strategy for Victory*, 105–7, 129–32.

41. Anthony Eden, secretary of state for war, memorandum, "Air Support for the Army," 23 September 1940, TNA AIR 20/3706.

42. RAF AP 3235, *Air Support*, 23–26.

43. "The Organisation, Function and Control of Airforces in Support of the Army in an Overseas Theatre of War," 21 May 1942, 1–2, TNA AIR 20/2812; Ministry of Information, *RAF Middle East: The Official Story of Air Operations in the Middle East, from February 1942 to January 1943* (London: HMSO, 1945), 7, 10; Lord Tedder, *With Prejudice* (London: Cassell, 1966), 211–12; John Connell, *Auchinleck: A Biography of Field-Marshal Sir Claude Auchinleck* (London: Cassell, 1959), 402, 411; and Col Andy Tjepkema, "Coningham: The Architect of Ground-Air Doctrine," *Air Clues* 45, no. 6 (June 1991): 205–8.

44. "Organisation, Functions and Control of Airforces"; "The Employment of Bombers and Fighter-Bombers in Co-operation with the Army," April 1944, TNA AIR 20/3213; and Ministry of Information, *RAF Middle East*, 12.

45. "Employment of Bombers," 2, TNA AIR 20/3213; Correspondence between Portal and Lord Tedder, 5 and 11 September 1941, Portal Papers, file 12, nos. 4 and 4a, Library of Christ Church College, Oxford; Tedder, *With Prejudice*, 163–4; Tedder, *Air Power in War* (London: Hodder and Stoughton, 1948), passim; and Terraine, foreword in Carrington, *Soldier at Bomber Command*, x.

46. Tedder, *With Prejudice*, 175–76, 187–90, 443–44; Tedder, *Air Power in War*, 91–92; Tedder to Portal, memorandum, 17 September 1941, Portal Papers, file 12, no. 5; and "The Value of a Centralised Air Force" (lecture 12), Trenchard Papers, MFC 76/1/357.

47. Air Marshal Sir Arthur Coningham, "The Development of Tactical Air Forces," *Journal of the Royal United Service Institute* 91 (1946): 211–26; Tjepkema, "Coningham," 205–6, 210; Vincent Orange, "The Commanders and the Command System," in *The End of the Beginning: A Symposium on the Land/ Air Co-operation in the Mediterranean War 1940–43*, Bracknell Paper no. 3 (UK: RAF Historical Society, 20 March 1992), 37–38, 43; and Orange, *Coningham* (London: Methuen, 1990), 81–83.

48. RAF AP 3235, *Air Support*, 64–65, TNA AIR 10/5547; "Organisation, Functions and Control of Airforces," 1–2, TNA AIR 20/2812; "The Middle East Campaigns," vol. 2, 289–92, and vol. 3, 93, TNA AIR 41/25 and 26; and Tjepkema, "Coningham," 205–6.

49. Along with the advent of the fighter-bomber came the final eclipse of the Stuka dive-bomber. As one contemporary and rather picturesque report stated, "The bogy of the dive-bomber had finally been exposed; when opposed by a determined fighter force it proved to be a crow masquerading in an eagle's feath-

ers." "Army Air Support," 49, TNA WO 277/34; and Richard P. Hallion, *Strike from the Sky* (Washington, DC: Smithsonian Institution Press, 1989), 156–57.

50. RAF AP 3235, *Air Support*, 64, TNA AIR 10/5547; "Army Air Support," 48, TNA WO 277/34; Ministry of Information, *RAF Middle East*, 14, 26–27; and Tjepkema, "Coningham," 207–8.

51. "Air Warfare—Training Instructions," 1941–42, Crerar Collection, box 103; and Peter Supf, *Luftwaffe von Sieg zu Sieg* (Berlin: Im Deutschen Verlag, 1941a). See also Joel Hayward, *Stopped at Stalingrad: The Luftwaffe and Hitler's Defeat in the East, 1942–43* (Lawrence, KS: University Press of Kansas, 1998); and James Corum, "The Luftwaffe's Army Support Doctrine, 1918–1941," *Journal of Military Affairs* 59 (January 1995): 53–76.

52. "Middle East Command HQ RAF Operational Record Book," March/April 1942, appendices, TNA AIR 24/1055 and 1082; and "Middle East Campaigns," vol. 2, 297–301, TNA AIR 41/25.

53. Tedder, *With Prejudice*, 404.

54. Elmhirst Papers, 6/6; and Orange, *Coningham*, 112.

55. James Lucas provides a succinct account of the "Gazala Gallop" in *War in the Desert: The Eighth Army at El Alamein* (London: Arms and Armour, 1982), 22–27. Detailed narratives can be read in I. S. O. Playfair et al., *The Mediterranean and Middle East*, vol. 3, *British Fortunes Reach Their Lowest Ebb* (London: HMSO, 1960), 223–97; Naill Barr, *Pendulum of War: The Three Battles of El Alamein* (London: Jonathon Cape, 2004); and Barrie Pitt, *Year of Alamein 1942* (London: Macmillan, 1986), 132–45.

56. General Auchinleck's Middle East despatch as quoted in "The Middle East Campaigns," vol. 4, 3–6, TNA AIR 41/50.

57. Extracts from 21st Panzer Division and Afrika Korps War Diaries as quoted in RAF AP 3235, *Air Support*, 68, TNA AIR 10/5547; "The Middle East Campaigns," vol. 3, 195–97, 202–3, and vol. 4, 2–6, TNA AIR 41/26 and 50; Air Ministry Private Office Papers, TNA AIR 19/557; and "Extracts from POW Statements: The Effectiveness of British Bombing," 12 July 1942, Portal Papers, file 12, no. 9. Rommel's observations on the deleterious effect the RAF's "continuous round-the-clock bombing" was having on his army can be read in B. H. Liddell Hart, ed., *The Rommel Papers* (London: Collins, 1953), 245, 260, 283–6; and Desmond Young, *Rommel* (London: Collins, 1950), 258–59, 272.

58. "The Middle East Campaigns," vol. 3, passim, TNA AIR 41/26; and John Terraine, *The Right of the Line* (London: Hodder and Stoughton, 1985), 370.

59. Tedder to Portal, memorandums, 6 February and 26 July 1942, Portal Papers, box C, file 8, nos. 14 and 24a; and Tedder, *With Prejudice*, 313–14.

60. "The Middle East Campaigns," vol. 3, 128, TNA AIR 41/26; Tedder to Portal, memorandums, 21 April and 29 June 1942, Portal Papers, box C, file 8, nos.18, 18a, 20; Tedder to Portal, memorandum, 12 July 1942, ibid., file 12, no. 9; and Tedder, *With Prejudice*, 305–6, 309–10.

61. Tedder to Portal, memorandums, 29 June and 16 July 1942, Portal Papers, box C, file 8, nos. 20 and 21; and "Middle East Campaigns," 4, 17, TNA AIR 41/50.

62. Terraine in the foreword to Carrington, *Soldier at Bomber Command*, x; and *End of the Beginning*, 65–66.

63. "The Middle East Campaigns," vol. 3, 224–27, TNA AIR 41/26; Ministry of Information, *RAF Middle East*, 72–82; and Air Historical Branch, RAF translations of German documents as quoted in Orange, *Coningham*, 99. For a detailed narrative of the First Battle of Alamein, see Playfair et al., *Mediterranean and Middle East*, vol. 3, 331–60; Lucas, *War in the Desert*, 29–38; Pitt, *Year of Alamein 1942*, 112–14, 202–4; and David Fraser, *Knight's Cross: A Life of Field Marshal Erwin Rommel* (London: Harper Collins, 1993), 347. Rommel's own impressions can be read in Hart, *Rommel Papers*, 243–53 and 327–29.

64. "The Middle East Campaigns," vol. 3, 226, and vol. 4, 3–4, 6, TNA AIR 41/26 and 50; "Air Ministry Private Office Papers," AIR 19/557; and R. T. Bickers, *The Desert Air War 1939–1945* (London: Leo Cooper, 1991), 93–97. For Rommel's precarious supply situation, the strategic significance of Malta as a base from which to disrupt Axis shipping, and the German High Command's decision to forgo subjugating the island prior to the "final" conquest of Egypt, see "The Middle East Campaigns," vol. 3, iii, 130–31, 195, and vol. 4, xxix, TNA AIR 41/26 and 50; and Playfair et al., *Mediterranean and Middle East*, vol. 3, 277–78, 325–30.

65. Tedder to Portal, memorandum, 16 July 1942, Portal Papers, box C, file 8, no. 21; and Tedder, *With Prejudice*, 312.

66. Tedder to Portal, memorandums, 25–26 July 1942, Portal Papers, box C, file 8, nos. 22a and 24a; Tedder, *With Prejudice*, 318–27; Correlli Barnett, *The Desert Generals*, 2nd ed. (London: Allen and Unwin, 1983), 231–39; and Lucas, *War in the Desert*, 40.

67. Lord Montgomery, *The Memoirs of Field Marshal the Viscount Montgomery of Alamein, K. G.* (London: Collins, 1958), 80–90, 99–100; Nigel Hamilton, *Monty: The Making of a General 1887–1942* (London: Hamish Hamilton, 1981), 606–25; David Fraser, *And We Shall Shock Them* (London: Hodder and Stoughton, 1983), 234–38; and Barnett, *Desert Generals*, 257–62.

68. Montgomery, *Memoirs*, 102; Tedder, *With Prejudice*, 347; and "Report on Visit to the Middle East by Air Marshal Sir Arthur Barratt, AOC Army Co-operation Command," August–September 1942, AIR 20/2106 and 37/760,

69. Elmhirst Papers, 6/2, vii, 14.

70. Hart, *Rommel Papers*, 285.

71. Playfair et al., *Mediterranean and Middle East*, vol. 4, *The Destruction of the Axis Forces in Africa* (London: HMSO, 1966), 33–34, 76; Marshal of the RAF Sir Arthur Tedder, "Air, Land and Sea Warfare," *Journal of the Royal United Service Institute* 91, no. 561 (February 1946): 59–68; Coningham, "Development of Tactical Air Forces," 214–15; and Fraser, *Knight's Cross*, 369, 375.

72. The RAF component under Air Marshal Sir William Walsh was designated Eastern Air Command. It covered Algeria east of Cape Tenes and provided support for the newly created First Army (a combined British and American force). The US Twelfth Air Force under Maj Gen James H. Doolittle, entitled Western Air Command, supported Maj Gen Lloyd Fredendall's American II Corps in western Algeria and the American forces of Maj Gen George S. Patton Jr. in Morocco. See W. F. Craven and J. L. Cate, *The Army Air Forces in World War II*, vol. 2 (Chicago: University of Chicago Press, 1948–1958), 41–66; George F. Howe, *Northwest Africa: Seizing the Initiative in the West*

(Washington, DC: Office of the Chief of Military History, US Army, 1957), 32–88; and Playfair et al., *Mediterranean and Middle East*, vol. 4, 110–28.

73. Daniel R. Mortensen, *A Pattern for Joint Operations* (Washington, DC: Office of Air Force History and US Army Center for Military History, 1987), 53, 56; Craven and Cate, *Army Air Forces*, 67–85; and David Syrett, "The Tunisian Campaign, 1942–43," in *Case Studies in the Development of Close Air Support*, ed. Cooling, 164.

74. Hallion, *Strike from the Sky*, 163.

75. Terraine, *Right of the Line*, 390–91; Mortensen, *Pattern for Joint Operations*, 50–56; and Orange, *Coningham*, 130.

76. RAF AP 3235, *Air Support*, 83, TNA AIR 10/5547; Mortensen, *Pattern for Joint Operations*, 59; and Syrett, "Tunisian Campaign," 164–67.

77. Tjepkema, "Coningham," 210.

78. "Middle East Campaigns," vol. 4, 471, TNA AIR 41/50; and Tedder, *With Prejudice*, 369.

79. Trenchard's memorandum on United Air Command, 20 December 1942, Portal Papers, folder 4, no.1; Tedder to Portal, 16 December 1942, Portal Papers, box C, file 8, no. 34; and Tedder, *With Prejudice*, 369–70.

80. Tedder, *With Prejudice*, 381.

81. Tedder to Portal, memorandum, December 1942, Portal Papers, folder 4, nos. 1, 1a; and MRAF Sir Arthur Tedder, "Air, Land and Sea Warfare," *Journal of the Royal United Service Institute* 91, no. 561 (February 1946): 59–68.

82. General Spaatz was appointed C-in-C of the Allied Air Forces in Northwest Africa on 5 January 1943, but not until 18 February was his new command made operational. See Playfair et al., *Mediterranean and Middle East*, vol. 4, 265, 271.

83. For full details on the restructuring of the Allied air forces in North Africa and the Mediterranean, including the major command appointments, see "Combined Chiefs of Staff, System of Air Command in the Mediterranean," 20 January 1943, TNA AIR 8/1035; RAF AP 3235, *Air Support*, 85–88, TNA AIR 10/5547; "Middle East Campaigns," 469–77, TNA AIR 41/50; and Playfair et al., *Mediterranean and Middle East*, vol. 4, 306–13.

84. For Rommel's surprise westward offensive toward the Kasserine Pass and the ignominious defeat of the US II Corps, see Martin Blumenson, *Kasserine Pass* (Boston: Houghton Mifflin Co., 1966).

85. Mortensen, *Pattern for Joint Operations*, 72–73; Hallion, *Strike from the Sky*, 171–72; Laurence S. Kuter, "Goddammit Georgie: North Africa, 1943: The Birth of TAC Doctrine," *Air Force Magazine* 56, no. 2 (February 1973): 51–56; and Orange, *Coningham*, 135–42. George Howe's *Northwest Africa: Seizing the Initiative in the West* (Washington, DC: Office of the Chief of Military History, Dept. of the Army, 1957), 492–95, gives the army view of reorganisation. For details on the creation of the 18th Army Group, see Playfair et al., *Mediterranean and Middle East*, vol. 4, 303–5.

86. Mortensen, *Pattern for Joint Operations*, 72–73; Coningham, "Development of Tactical Air Forces," 215; and Syrett, "Tunisian Campaign," 174, 178–79.

87. US War Department, Field Manual (FM) 100-20, *Command and Employment of Air Power*, 21 July 1943, 1, 10–11; Mortensen, *Pattern for Joint*

Operations, 77–83; Hallion, *Strike from the Sky*, 172–75; and Robert Futrell, *Ideas, Concepts, Doctrine: A History of Basic Thinking in the United States Air Force* (Maxwell AFB, AL: Air University Press, 1971, 1989), 69.

88. C. E. Carrington, "Army/Air Co-operation, 1939–1943," *Journal of the Royal United Service Institute* 115 (December 1970): 40; Carrington, *Soldier at Bomber Command*, 11; and "Army/Air Co-operation," Carrington Papers, 81/11/6.

89. US War Department FM 100-20, *Command and Employment of Air Power*, 21 July 1943; and William R. Burt, *Adventures with Warlords* (New York: Vantage Press, 1994), 147–48.

90. Tedder, *Air Power in War*, 11. This book was based on a series of four lectures Tedder gave at Cambridge University, The Lees Knowles Lectures, delivered in February and March 1947.

91. Montgomery, *Memoirs*, 102; Tedder, *With Prejudice*, 347; "Report on Visit to the Middle East by Air Marshal Sir Arthur Barratt, AOC Army Co-operation Command," August–September 1942, TNA AIR 20/2106 and 37/760.

92. TNA CAB 79/60 COS(43)91(0), 1 May 1943; and "Army-Air Co-operation," 76, TNA CAB 101/136.

93. "Exercise 'Spartan': GHQ [General Headquarters] Home Forces Combined Exercise," December 1942—March 1943, TNA AIR 16/559; "Exercise 'Spartan': General Arrangements," January—March 1943, TNA AIR 39/91; and "Exercise 'Spartan': Reports," March—May 1943, TNA AIR 39/118.

94. The First Tactical Air Force was in fact the Western Desert Air Force, although the title was never used officially. By naming the new UK air formation the Second TAF, however, the Air Staff honoured the invaluable work of the WDAF in developing an effective air support system. For the formation of the Second TAF, see "Tactical Air Force Command: Formation in the United Kingdom," 1943, TNA AIR 2/7808; "Tactical Air Force: Formation (May–October 1943)," TNA AIR 8/988; and RAF AP 3235, *Air Support*, 43–45, TNA AIR, 10/5547. The Canadian contribution to the formation of the Second TAF is described in Bereton Greenhous et al., *The Crucible of War, 1939–1945: The Official History of the Royal Canadian Air Force*, vol. 3 (Toronto: University of Toronto Press in Co-operation with the Dept. of National Defence and the Canadian Govt. Pub. Centre, Supply and Services, Canada, 1994), 248–64.

95. Dean, *Royal Air Force and Two World Wars*, 215.

96. Wing Cdr Harv Smyth, RAF, "From Coningham to Project Coningham-Keyes," *Air Power Review* 10, no.1 (Spring 2007): 1.

97. Ibid.

98. Loden, "E-mails from Helmand."

99. Ibid.

100. House of Commons (HC) Defence Committee, HC 635, *Lessons of Iraq: Government Response to the Committee's Third Report of Session 2003–04*, 8 June 2004 (London: The Stationery Office Limited, 2004), 9; and Smyth, "From Coningham to Project Coningham-Keyes," 17–19.

101. See David Ian Hall, ed., "The Relevance and Role of Military History, Battlefield Tours and Staff Rides for Armed Forces in the 21st Century," *Defence Studies* 5, no. 1 (March 2005); and Capt Gilles Van Nederveen, USAF,

retired, and Daniel R. Mortensen, "Air Staff Rides: Wartime Leadership Experience," *Air and Space Power Journal* 16, no. 4 (Winter 2002): 25–26.

102. HCSC, "Staff Ride," 3–12 April 2006.

103. Churchill's Middle East directive on air support was later published as Middle East Training Pamphlet (Army and RAF) no. 3, *Direct Air Support*, 30 September 1941. See Hall, *Strategy for Victory*, 108, and appendix, 157–72.

104. "Improving Training in the Air Environment" (unclassified presentation ACOS A7, Air Land Conference, UK Defence Academy, 30 August 2007).

Abbreviations

AASF	Advanced Air Striking Force
AHB	Air Historical Branch
AOC	air officer commander/commanding
AOC-in-C	air officer commander in chief
ASC	air-support controls
BAFF	British Air Forces in France
BEF	British Expeditionary Force
C2	command and control
CIGS	chief of the Imperial General Staff
C-in-C	commander in chief
COS	chief of staff
GHQ	general headquarters
HCSC	Higher Command and Staff College
HQME	headquarters, Middle East
JALO	Joint Air-Land Organisation
KCL	King's College, London
NATAF	Northwest African Tactical Air Force
NWAAF	Northwest African Air Forces
PC-K	Project Coningham-Keyes
RAF	Royal Air Force
RFC	Royal Flying Corps
RNAS	Royal Naval Air Service
RPG	rocket-propelled grenade
TAF	tactical air force
3 PARA	3rd Battalion, The Parachute Regiment
UK	United Kingdom
WDAF	Western Desert Air Force